T0158522

LESSONS
FROM
THE WILD

By
Shayamal Vallabhjee

New Chapter Media

Published in 2011 by
New Chapter Press
1175 York Ave Suite #3s
New York
Tel: +1 703-567-5076
www.NewChapterMedia.com

ISBN: 978-0-942257-85-4

Editorial Consultant: Lisa Henman & Meghan McHugh
Cover Design: Kirsten Navin
Illustrations: KS Designers
Design & Layout: KS Designers

Distributed by: Independent Publishers Group
www.IPGBook.com

Printed in the United States

Dedicated To
HIS HOLINESS BHAKTI CHARU SWAMI
*(My Eternal Spiritual Master who has been ever
so patient in guiding me)*

CONTENTS

Contents

FOREWORD

In over 20 years of competing on a professional platform, I have seen it all. There is the tireless dedication, clinical mental toughness, superior physical durability, and unparalleled love for the game that is ultimately required to enjoy successes that result in podium performances. The road ahead is never easy but it is the enthusiasm of the individual that sets him apart from his peers.

The word enthusiasm has come from the ancient word "entheos," which means "fire of the gods." The word is fire — not charisma or charm, which are all too easy to mimic. But fire, a burning motivating force which when possessed by the right person can create a truly inspired vision, which results in goals attainable at will. The fire I speak off is a sacred fire that is infectious and inspirational.

Four years ago, I encountered a similar fire personified through the boundless energy displayed by this book's author Shayamal Vallabhjee. Both as a physical therapist and a motivator, he was truly remarkable. Shayamal was the epitome of motivation and inspiration whose vision ran deep. I have been fortunate enough to witness this inspired flame, which was forged in the furnace of achievement and affliction, grow and touch the lives on many through his work and his writing.

Lessons from the Wild is a simple, easy read that is both warm and inspiring. Shayamal has brilliantly symbolized the challenges wild animals face and our own adversities. In professional sport, it's all about "finding a way" to achieve your goal and claim victory. I have always used words like determination, persistence, courage and sacrifice to best explain what makes a champion, but upon reading *Lessons from the Wild*, I have a new found respect and a deeper understanding of what these words truly mean.

Lessons from the Wild opened my mind to a whole new world — a world where self-belief, preparation, confidence, determination, integrity and trust take on new meaning. A place where indecision is the difference between life and death, and a world that truly is best described as "Survival of the Fittest." But most importantly, it has opened my eyes to the unknown world of wild animals and their lifelong struggles.

Mahesh Bhupathi
Wimbledon, French and US Open
Doubles Champion

INTRODUCTION

I have been through a lot and have suffered a great deal. But I have had lots of happy moments, as well. Every moment in one's life is different from the other. The good, the bad, hardships, the joy, the tragedy, love and happiness are all interwoven into a single indescribable whole that is called LIFE. You cannot separate the good from the bad. And perhaps there is no need to do so, either.
– Jacquelyn Kennedy Onassis

Life is a journey. A journey that sometimes leads us into perilous situations with little to no hope of success. A journey that will at times require courage, strength and fortitude to overcome adversity. A journey that is a struggle speckled only with moments of joy, laughter and happiness – but moments that have the power to take our breath away, and make the journey worthwhile.

The animal kingdom has a cross-spectrum of millions of species of land, air and aquatic life. These animals co-exist in a diverse environment that constantly poses a threat to their daily survival, as well as a threat to the existence of their species. The battles and hardships we face on a day-to-day basis are lifelong struggles in the animal world. *Lessons from the Wild* is a unique collection of adaptations, migratory patterns and stories of hardship that have molded the animal kingdom into a silent reservoir of guts and glory, beyond our wildest comprehension.

Let *Lessons from the Wild* guide you into the world of animals, and let the animals show us the meaning of life and motivate us to overcome the challenges of everyday life.

Teamwork

*The co-operative or coordinated effort on the part
of a group or persons acting as a team or in
the interests of a common cause*

The Story of the Snow Geese

The snow goose is a medium-sized goose that spends the winter near the Gulf of Mexico. Each year they embark on a mammoth journey across North America to the Arctic Tundra. Five million geese make this journey each year, which is almost 3000 miles long. It's a three-month epic journey, which will bear witness to an exhilarating display of teamwork and camaraderie. The Arctic Tundra is the perfect breeding ground and this makes the migration worth the effort.

The flight patterns of the snow geese have been studied extensively for many years. Some extraordinary findings in their flight and behavioral patterns have over the years formed the cornerstones in teamwork fundamentals. Here are a few:

- As each goose flaps its wings it creates "uplift" for the birds that follow. By flying in a V-formation, the whole flock adds 72% greater flying range than if each bird flew alone.

- When a goose falls out of formation, it suddenly feels the drag and resistance of flying alone. It quickly moves back into formation to take advantage of the lifting power of the bird immediately in front of it.

- The geese honk from behind to encourage those up front to keep up their speed.

- When a goose gets sick, wounded, or shot down, two geese drop out of formation and follow it down to help and protect it. They stay with it until it dies or is able to fly again. Then, they launch out with another formation or catch up with the flock.

The story of the snow geese helps us focus our attention on the timeless principle of teamwork. The acronym for teamwork is: *Together Everyone Achieves More*, which is not only apt but also instrumental in highlighting how important the need is for all individuals to pool together their respective talents and align their actions towards the unified goal of the group. Teamwork is a cornerstone principle in all-successful businesses, organizations and sports teams, but is underlined by each individual's commitment, determination, hunger to overcome adversity and their respect for each member of the team. The snow geese are wonderful examples of teamwork and camaraderie. They would never accomplish their migration to the Arctic Tundra without the collective effort of each goose. The snow geese migration best exemplifies teamwork and the underlying principle of strength in numbers.

Courage

Strength in the face of pain or grief

The Story of the Bottlenose Dolphin

Shark Bay lies on the extreme western coast of Australia, approximately 497 miles from Perth. The arid landscape of Shark Bay, combined with many peninsulas, islands and bays, creates a great diversity of landscapes and seascapes that are exceptionally scenic. It is a spectacle of nature that is home to many varieties of fauna, flora and animals that are both sea and land dwelling.

Of all the inhabitants of Shark Bay, the most common visitor is the Indian Ocean bottlenose dolphin. The Indo-Pacific bottlenose dolphin has a rich dark-grey color with a subtle tint of light grey on its belly. It can grow to about 8.5 feet long and can weigh up to 507 lbs.

These dolphins have developed certain behavioral and feeding patterns that are unique to the Shark Bay Indo-Pacific bottlenose dolphin. They have adopted a unique fishing style

known as "hydroplaning" in shallow water. The fish in Shark Bay have been found to swim in extremely shallow waters, making them tantalizingly out of reach. The dolphins using this hydroplaning technique are now able to catch fish that would normally be unattainable.

Hydroplaning is a different, but risky, shallow water hunting strategy used by dolphins in Shark Bay. Hydroplaning involves vigorously pumping the tail in order to generate momentum and speed that will carry the dolphin through the shallow waters, enabling them to catch fish. A dolphin must consider a number of factors (speed, depth and likelihood of success) before deciding whether or not to make a run for a fish being sought.

In life, we face many challenges, which by nature are opportunities to make mistakes. These mistakes are inevitable stepping-stones in our development. It is important to remember that a failure is only an event and by no measure an indication of whom we are. Mistakes and failures are marks of courage. They remind us that we were courageous enough to make and stick by our decision.

As a wise man once said, *"It's better to have tried and failed than never to have tried at all."*

The hydroplaning technique used by the Shark Bay dolphins poses the obvious real threat of being beached. They are seldom successful on the first few attempts but their courage in the face of adversity is often handsomely rewarded. The bottlenose dolphin is a prime example of how courage can overcome adversity.

*"Few are they who have had a chance to achieve happiness - and fewer those who have taken that chance." – **Andre Maurois***

SOLITUDE

A state of being or living alone

The Story of the Pinta Island Tortoise (Lonesome George)

The Galápagos Islands are situated in the Pacific Ocean some 621 miles from the South American continent. These 19 islands and the surrounding marine reserve have been uniquely named the 'living museum and showcase of evolution'. Located at a confluence of three ocean currents, the Galápagos Islands are a "melting pot" of marine species. It is a haven of wildlife and a UNESCO World Heritage Site.

The Galápagos Islands are also home to the rarest animal on earth. A giant Pinta Island Tortoise more affectionately known as Lonesome George currently lives in the Charles Darwin Research Centre on Santa Cruz Island. Lonesome George is the only giant Pinta Island tortoise in existence. By estimation, he is 80 years old and weighs in at 200 lbs.

For the past fifteen years, scientists have been trying to get

Lonesome George to mate, but efforts have been futile. They have introduced two tortoises of different sub-species into his pen, but George has been in no hurry to procreate. Last year, Lonesome George mated for the first time in his 36 years in captivity. Unfortunately the eggs laid by one female were infertile. Lonesome George was deprived of all company at an early age and has spent the last three decades alone. Despite a life of complete solitude, he is solely responsible for the future of his species. When he dies, the Pinta Island tortoise will be extinct.

"Solitude is the furnace of transformation. Without solitude we remain victims of our society and continue to be entangled in the illusions of the false self." – Henri J.N. Nouwen

Solitude is a chosen state of being. It's an all empowering state that re-affirms ones self competence through reflection and contemplation. It's a form of personal nourishment that comes from oneself, which is integral for mental growth and stability, personal assessment, and the opportunity to allow your creative juices to flow. But most importantly, solitude leaves you with nothing but yourself and it is in that state that's one's true self is exposed. It's where you become conscious of your own thoughts and experiences, and from here true personal growth is born.

*"Solitude shows us what should be, society shows us what we are." – **Robert Cecil***

SACRIFICE

*Giving up something of value for
the sake of something else*

The Story of the North Pacific Salmon

The Pacific salmon is characterized by beauty, grace and elegance. These anadromous fish have a silvery sheen with spotted backs and fins. The Pacific salmon is born in fresh water rivers, before they make the long journey to the salt-waters of the North Pacific Ocean to live their lives to maturity.

The Pacific salmon are born in gravel beds in fresh water streams anywhere from a hundred yards to a thousand miles from the sea. After a few months of incubation, the eggs hatch into alevins, before emerging to the surface as inch long fry's. They will then spend anywhere from six months to a year growing in the fresh waters before heading downstream to the ocean in spring.

The Pacific salmon will spend most of its life in the salt waters of the Pacific Ocean, where they will feed abundantly for the better part of five years. As they approach maturity, the

salmon will navigate themselves upstream, using only their sense of smell, to the freshwaters in which they were born.

The struggle upstream can last anything from a few weeks to a few months, as they battle a variety of obstacles like rapids, falls, rocks, fallen logs, and predators. During this entire journey the salmon will not feed but rely solely on stored body fats, as they battle against time to reach the spawning grounds where they were once born.

In the placid waters of their birth, the female will lay her eggs. The male will then fertilize these eggs before covering them with a milky substance called milt. The long journey upstream is a race against time and obstacles, which unfortunately culminates in death. Shortly after the spawning period, the salmon will die and its body will drift downstream.

"If you want to do something badly enough, have the patience to realize that minor setbacks on the road to the end are just that — minor." - **Gary Player**

Sacrifice goes hand in hand with knowledge, confidence and trust in the process. Sometimes it may seem that we experience more disappointments than victories, and at times we find it hard to give ourselves a reason to continue. But if you chose to take on whatever comes your way with a positive attitude and an unwavering commitment to your goal, you will have increased your possibility of success by 100%. Mistakes are inevitable and sacrifices are the seeds we sow that will one day flourish into flowers of appreciation and happiness.

The North Pacific salmon is an inspiring example of sacrifice. They make a grueling journey against testing climatic conditions with the threat of predators and time. All for the reason of procreation, despite the end result being death. The North Pacific salmon represents the ultimate sacrifice and serves as a lesson as to how giving up something to reach a goal can be our greatest achievement.

"If a man hasn't discovered something that he will die for, he isn't fit to live." – **Martin Luther King, Jr.**

ALTRUISM

Unselfish concern for others

The Story of the Lioness

The lion has always been known as the King of the Jungle, and traditionally associated with strength, courage, royalty, authority, dominance and power. The lion is the second largest of all cat species and can measure up to 8 ½ feet, excluding the tail, and weigh up to 550lbs.

The lion is the only truly social cat, living in groups called prides. A pride generally consists of more females than males. The main role of the males in the pride is to defend their territory and protect the cubs. It is the lioness that is responsible for most duties within a pride.

A lioness is 20-35% smaller than a male. They are the primary hunters in a pride, and execute their skills with precision and complex teamwork. The kill is generally shared between all members of the pride, with the males eating first.

A lioness will give birth to between 2-4 cubs. A lion cub is born blind, and is completely dependant on the mother. This makes them extremely vulnerable. In order to protect the cubs, the lioness will leave the pride with her cubs. For the next six weeks, she will care for them in the wild. The lioness will hunt to feed the young, and serve as the only protection for them. She also displays her unselfishness by often caring for cubs which are not her own. For weeks, she will lead a nomadic lifestyle to avoid predators and other prides. The cubs will only be introduced into the pride after six weeks.

"You have got to think about the 'big things' while you are doing the small things, so that all the small things go in the right direction." – **Alvin Toffler**

The life of a lioness is a constant battle. She struggles to support the pride, and in her most vulnerable state after giving birth, she endures the hardships of the wild alone with her young. The lionesses struggle is her investment. If she does not think about the future, she won't have a future. Strategic planning, foresight and integral investments are key business principles that draw a parallel symbolism to the altruistic behavior of the lioness. The male lion may be the king of the jungle, but it is the sacrifice and unselfishness of the female that has allowed the lion species to survive. The lioness and her unselfish devotion to her young exemplifies what being a parent is all about.

"Happy are those who dream dreams and are ready to pay the price to make them come true." – L.J. Cardinal Suenens

PERSEVERANCE

*Continue in a course of action in spite
of difficulty or lack of success*

The Story of the Emperor Penguin

Every year as winter approaches, a group of animals begins a remarkable journey. The emperor penguin, the largest penguin species on earth, will migrate deep into the Antarctica and endure the harshest winter on earth in order to procreate.

Each year this journey will begin with a seemingly endless swim in the icy cold Atlantic waters. They will reach pressure points 40 times greater than any surface pressure, and withstand conditions far more traumatic that most sea dwelling animals will ever encounter. During the swim, its heart rate will drop to five beats per minute, and all non-essential organs will shut down to ensure longer swims and less energy consumption. This grueling trip culminates in a 60 mile walk across the frozen terrain of Antarctica. For 20 days and 20 nights they will march to a remote land that supports no other life on earth. And here they will begin to search for a partner.

The emperor penguin is monogamous. They will have only one mate, and remain completely faithful. In the harshest winter on earth the emperor penguin will breed, withstanding temperatures below 40 degrees Celsius and icy winds over 60 mph. When the egg is hatched, the female will begin her journey back to the Atlantic waters to feed. The male will remain behind to face the worst conditions imaginable. For 64 days, the male Emperor Penguin will incubate the egg enduring temperatures below 60 degrees Celsius with winds over 100 mph. No other animal on earth suffers such a fate. The egg that rests upon the feet of the penguin can at no point touch the icy surface, as the young would freeze upon contact. They will spend a total of 115 days fasting and huddling together, to give birth to a single new life. The female only returns after the hatching process is complete, fully nourished and able to feed the young.

"Four steps to achievement: plan purposefully, prepare prayerfully, proceed positively, pursue persistently."
– William A. Ward

Success in the face of adversity is underlined by good discipline, determination, hunger and focus regardless of the circumstances. This is an age-old philosophy that is apparently clear in most successful businesses and sporting teams. The emperor penguin is a shining example of the perseverance and dedication required to achieve success. They endure more hardship than any other living organism and overcome obstacles beyond our wildest comprehension, for the single goal of procreation. The emperor penguin has taught us that we can achieve anything if we persevere. Remember, "there is no success without effort. There is no reward without hard work."

"Diamonds are lumps of coal that stuck to their jobs."
– B.C. Forbes

INDEPENDENCE

*Freedom from the control, support,
aid or the like of others*

The Story of the Anaconda

Anacondas are the largest and strongest non-venomous snakes in the world, averaging between 25-35 feet in length and 12 inches in diameter. They are semi aquatic snakes which belong to the Boa Constrictor family. Found mostly in the rivers and waters of the Amazon in tropical South America, anacondas are fast becoming known for their reputation to consume large animal's whole. Although they are snakes, the anaconda does not have fangs. They are strong enough to overpower their prey, and generally kill their prey by suffocation or drowning.

An anaconda will reach sexual maturity in 3-4 years. At that time the females will give off a scent that will attract males. Generally the strongest male will win the fight and mate with the female. The gestation period of an anaconda is nearly 6 months, following which the female will give birth to between

20-50 living young snakes. An anaconda snake is completely independent from birth. The young will slither off immediately after birth in search of food and will continue to fend for themselves for the duration of their lifespan.

"*The only man who makes no mistakes is the man who never does anything.*" – **Eleanor Roosevelt**

In life as in business, independence is an attribute of a leader. We are all on our path to finding equilibrium, and accepting that our lives with have ups and downs. The most important aspect is that we learn and gain strength from our failures. Doing this will ensure that one day we will surpass our own considerable expectations and be amazed at what we have accomplished. Being independent means being critical and accepting accountability whilst remaining committed, because the successes you will enjoy are the result of your clarity of thought and focus.

The anaconda is one of those rare species that live a life of solitude with absolutely no parental care at all. They are totally and completely independent from birth to death, and best illustrate the benefits and strength found in being independent and free from the control of others.

"*The man who makes everything that leads to happiness depend upon himself, and not upon other men, has adopted the very best plan for living happily.*" – **Plato**

UNCERTAINTY

Lack of assurance in a situation

The Story of the Wildebeest and the Serengeti Migration

The journey of the wildebeest is part of the greatest wildlife spectacle on earth. The Great Serengeti Migration is the largest land migration on earth. Over 1.5 million wildebeest and 300,000 zebras and antelope migrate each year from the Serengeti Plains to the green grassy hills of Kenya's Masai Mara National Reserve. It's a 1,800-mile journey in search of green grass and water, the life source for every single wildebeest.

The banks of the Mara River is the scene of one of the greatest dramas on earth. With each passing day, the herds of wildebeest draw closer to the banks. In time, huge numbers of wildebeest will be present, waiting for an opportune moment to attempt their crossing. It's never an easy decision, especially for the few up front. The arriving wildebeest are constantly forcing the herd forward, and the waters of the Mara River are far from welcoming. Africa's deadliest predators are waiting.

The crossings are inevitable. As the herds cross, crocodiles are lying in wait for any weak and feeble young that can't cope with the strong currents, or lose their mothers. On either side of the river, leopards, lions, wild dogs, and hyenas have also gathered to feast on weak and injured wildebeest. This is the most testing moment these wildebeest will face in their journey to the lush pastures of Masai Mara Reserve.

The wildebeest herds have always sought refuge in numbers. Unfortunately the huge numbers that attempt the crossing of the Mara River are sometimes detrimental. More wildebeest will die in the stampede across the river than by the predators. Each year 250,000 wildebeest will not survive this journey.

"Knowledge and effort help people go on rather than give up. Perseverance is the willingness to stay in just a little longer, run just a few more steps, practice just a little harder, try just one more time. The difference between success and failure if often how long people give it before they give up." – **Rosabeth Moss Kanter**

Life is a constant challenge that will always be a work in progress and a never-ending story of not giving up. Part of the growth process is understanding your challenges and approaching them with a positive attitude. In life and business, 90% of the battle is mental. If you believe in yourself and in your ability to overcome any obstacle, then you have set in motion a chain reaction of events that will shift the paradigm grossly in your favour.

The life of a wildebeest is an endless pilgrimage in search of water and green grass. There is no end, but only a life of uncertainty and struggle. The Serengeti Wildebeest has shown us that although life may be a constant struggle and be full of uncertainty, the strong will survive and ultimately overcome adversity.

"Success is to be measured not so much by the position that one has reached in life as by the obstacles he has overcome trying to succeed." – **Booker T. Washington**

STRATEGY

A detailed plan for achieving a goal

The Story of the Octopus and the Squid

Squid and octopus are deep sea dwelling molluscs. They are taxonomic relatives of the garden snail and slug but display a completely different set of behavioral adaptations.

These wonderful sea dwellers have a particularly unique behavioral technique that doubles up as an effective escape strategy against predators. In the intestine region of these animals, there is a special sac-like organ that contains a gland that secretes a brown or black liquid, rich in the pigment melanin. The liquid is more commonly known as ink.

When threatened, these animals have the ability to compress the "ink" sac and squirt the liquid from its anus. This liquid suspends itself in the surrounding water, giving off the appearance of a dummy squid, commonly known as a pseudomorph. This pseudomorph attracts and momentarily holds the attention of the predator, while the octopus or squid

escapes. What is even more remarkable is that thin species of octopus produce thin pseudomorphs whilst more round species produce rounder clouds of ink.

Certain species of squid inhabit deep ocean waters, where very little light is available. In their cases, the ink pseudomorph would be of little help against the backdrop of the dark murky surroundings. These species have further adapted themselves to secrete luminescent ink that creates a flash of light that is said to confuse the predator for just long enough to effect a successful escape.

"Good fighters of the old first put themselves beyond the possibility of defeat, and then waited for an opportunity of defeating the enemy." – Sun Tzu

A strategy is a plan devised from a detailed analysis of the strength and weaknesses of yourself and your obstacles. It does not guarantee success but ensures you are prepared for the opportunity. It is your roadmap for success and an integral component in achieving our goals. In fact it separates the best from the rest in all aspects of life and business.

The octopus and its use of a pseudomorph to deceive is one of the most ingenious plans to have evolved from the wild. They have adequately displayed how strategy, which has been a cornerstone principle in business and military for generations, can be equally effective in nature.

*"Failing to plan is planning to fail." – **Alan Lakein***

DECEPTION

The art of deceiving

The Story of the Viceroy Butterfly

The viceroy butterfly is an orange and black North American butterfly. This Mullerian Mimic of the monarch butterfly is much smaller with a wingspan of between 53-81 mm.

The monarch butterfly has a very brightly colored orange and black outer appearance, which serves as a warning to predators. The viceroy butterfly being a Mullerian Mimic to the monarch has a very similar appearance, with the only noticeable distinction being a postmedian black line that runs across the veins on the hindwing.

The viceroy butterfly in its caterpillar stage feeds on trees in the willow family Salicaceae. They sequester the salicylic acid in their bodies, which makes them bitter, and upsets predators' stomachs. The monarch butterfly has a renowned reputation for being distasteful and poisonous, and uses its brightly coloured appearance as a warning signal to any lurking predators. The

viceroy butterfly has over time transformed itself to mimic the outward appearance of the monarch butterfly and deceive any predators that may threaten their existence.

"All warfare is based on deception. Hence, when able to attack, we must seem unable; when using our forces, we must seem inactive; when we are near, we must make the enemy believe we are far away; when far away, we must make him believe we are near." - **Sun Tzu**

Deception is a survival technique in the wild that has prevented the extinction of many species of life, allowing them to co-exist in a mutualistic environment. This technique has also been replicated in many successful military operations for centuries. Deception involves developing a deep understanding of your obstacles, and how best to leverage that. In life, a very similar understanding is required to forge relationships with both friend and foe. The vicerory butterfly is an example of such brilliance. Whilst deception is not generally regarded as something to aspire to, in certain circumstances it is necessary to ensure survival.

As the age old saying goes, "*Keep your friends close and your enemies closer.*"

FAITH

Complete trust or confidence in something

The Story of the Basilisk Lizard

The green basilisk lizard, more affectionately known as The "Jesus Christ Lizard," is abundant in the tropical rain forests of Central America. The basilisk lizard, which is part of the iguana family, spends much of its life in trees not far from bodies of water. These omnivorous lizards grow to roughly two feet in length and survive on a diet comprised primarily of plant material, small vertebrates, insects and fruit.

The basilisk lizard acquired its nickname The "Jesus Christ Lizard" because of its unique ability to run on water. When threatened these lizards can drop from trees onto bodies of water, and run at about five feet per second across the surface of the water.

The basilisk is able to perform this task because of their long toes on their rear feet that have webbed skin that unfurls in the water. The increased surface area, coupled

with rapid feet movements, create tiny pockets of air that prevent them from sinking. They can run on the surface of water for roughly 15 feet before gravity eventually takes over. The basilisk then relies on their excellent swimming skills to steer themselves to safety.

*"Confidence is easier to define than it is to measure. It is an assuredness in one's ability to accomplish a task even under the most stressful circumstances." – **Tiger Woods***

Faith is a product of self confidence which is a product of preparation. Confidence comes from applying knowledge successfully in preparation. That confidence helps instil a faith in the process, and that faith is what we subconsciously rely on in times of danger. It's what helps eliminate the fear of failure by reaffirming that we have chosen the correct process based on the successes we previously enjoyed.

Many animals live in water but only the Basilisk Lizard can run on water. This unique skill has some very obvious dangers, but the basilisk's complete faith and trust in their ability to successfully perform that skill under pressure is admirable and shows how having faith and confidence in our own abilities can enable us to achieve the impossible.

"Let us train our minds to desire what the situation demands."
– Marcus Annaeus Seneca

LOVE

To have a profoundly tender affection for someone

The Story of the Japanese Shield Bug

One of the most endearing examples of love and devotion are found in the maternal instincts and behavior patterns of a small group of insects. The Japanese shield bug, indigenous to the forests of Japan's south islands, is a brilliant red and black bug.

These tiny insects entire existence depends on a completely unreliable source of food called drupes. Drupes are small fleshy fruit that fall from one kind of tree, during a particular time of the year. These fruit are so rare, that evolution has forced the breeding period of these little bugs to coincide with the falling of the fruit.

As if this is not difficult enough, the shield bug which makes its home in leaves, is forced to take shelter about 40-50 feet from these trees because the Olacaceae tree does not shed its leaves simultaneously with the ripening of its fruit.

This means the nest will have to be established a few meters away and specially selected ripened fruit will have to be carried to the nest. Only 5% of all drupes that fall are worthy enough to be eaten. Each drupe weighs three times the weight of the bug. This process in itself presents many threats, as other less dedicated mothers often ambush the bug. Some even resort to stealing drupes from unattended nests.

A successful nest will require close to 150 drupes to help nurture the young to independence. To make matters even worse, the young themselves are very temperamental. If they feel that the mother is not providing them with a healthy supply of good drupes, they will leave to join another nest, where they will be welcomed openly. A dedicated mother who cannot find good drupes for her young will make the ultimate sacrifice. She will provide her body as food for her young. Even in successful nests she will be their last meal before reaching independence.

*"Love bears all things, believes all things, hopes all things, endures all things." – **Corinthians 13:17***

One of most important components of preparing to succeed is maintaining a healthy balance in life. An integral part of that healthy balance focuses on nurturing holistic relationships with your family, friends and colleagues. Their love and support are vital rungs on the ladder of success. Love needs to be cherished, preserved and never taken for granted because love may ultimately be the difference between life and death or mediocrity and excellence. The shield bug's devotion, care and dedication to raising her young successfully is the greatest example of love in the animal kingdom and is something we should all aspire to. Her sacrifice of life in the name of love is truly inspiring.

*"Passion makes the world go round. Love just makes it a safer place." – **Ice T***

FEARLESSNESS

Acting without fear; being brave and bold

The Story of the Honey Badger

The honey badger, which is indigenous throughout Africa and parts of Asia, is a small animal with a very distinct appearance. This furry animal has a predominantly blackish brown body and face with a whitish grey head and back. Weighing in at between 20-30 lbs, these conspicuous carnivores have earned themselves the title "The most fearless animal in the world".

The honey badger, an intelligent animal that is seldom preyed on gets it ferocious reputation from its tendency to attack animals much larger than itself. These unassuming animals are very nomadic and solitary, and their aggressive tendencies make them even more dangerous. The honey badger will prey upon anything from earthworms, scorpions, porcupines and hares to squirrels, meerkats and mongooses. They have also been known to attack and kill tortoises, one-metre long crocodiles, young gazelles and snakes – both venomous and non-venomous.

Animals even as large as lions, tigers, bear and wolves hardly ever attack the ferocious honey badger. They have a thick yet loose skin that allows them to maneuver easily and launch a counter-attack at will.

"Standing on the defensive indicates insufficient strength; attacking, a superabundance of strength." – **Sun Tzu**

Fearlessness is all about attitude – our mental approach to the task at hand. Life will always present us with challenges because that is a by-product of an evolving species. Understanding that winners face up to these challenges is the first step to developing a mental toughness that's required to produce a champion.

"If you don't find a way, you will find an excuse." – **Anonymous**

The honey badger is a killing machine that has aptly earned the title "most fearless animal in the world". This title only comes from a reputation for being ruthless in battle, irrespective of the size of your opponent and the potential danger you may face. This inconspicuous animal has taught us that although the road ahead may not be an easy one, a positive attitude is everything.

"*I quit being afraid when my first venture failed and the sky didn't fall down.*" – **Allen H. Nueharth**

EFFORT

An exertion of physical or mental power

The Story of the Beaver

The beaver, "Nature's Greatest Engineer", is the second largest rodent in the world. These primarily nocturnal, semi-aquatic animals have poor eyesight but navigate themselves very well with their keen sense of hearing, smell and touch. A very distinguishable feature of the beaver is their four prominent front teeth that are used to chop down trees. These chisel like teeth are exceptional tools for felling trees, and are one of the beaver's greatest assets.

Over time, the beaver has earned himself the nickname "Nature's Greatest Engineer" purely because of their ability to reconstruct surrounding wetlands like rivers and streams into dams. Using their large front teeth and powerful paws, they construct these dams with large logs, filled in between with small branches and weeds, before being pasted together with mud. It is a grueling process that not only takes time but physical stamina as well.

Protection is the primary reason for their dam building. A beaver's abode is a lodge created with an underwater entrance. Linked to this lodge is an intricate series of paths that will allow the beaver to transport food and raw materials around the entire area. Beavers work most often at night. Any damages to their dam walls are seldom left unattended for more than 24 hours. The beaver's overwhelming discipline and dedication to preserving their surrounding environment, despite the physically enduring work required, is conducive to the flourishing of their species.

"Opportunities are usually disguised as hard work, so most people don't recognize them." - Ann Landers

Developing goals and having strategic plans to overcome life's adversities is the first step to achieving success. The second and most crucial step is to have the work ethic and drive required to see your goals to fruition.

"Success is peace of mind or self satisfaction knowing you did your best to become the best you are capable of becoming."
- *John Wooden*

The acronym for HARD work is: Hunger, Attitude, Resilience, and Discipline in your work ethic. This clearly spells out the secret to success that is appropriately applicable in any field in business, sport and life. There are no short cuts to success and everything we wish to achieve in life is inadvertently "just outside our comfort zone."

The beaver "Nature's engineer" is without doubt a shining example of how hard work and effort in the face of adversity will ultimately be rewarded.

STRENGTH

Force in numbers

The Story of the African Driver Ant

Deep in the forests of West Africa lives the most unassuming killing machine known to man. Measuring in at between 0.5-1,5 cm in length, the driver ant is a slow moving, silent and deadly inhabitant of the forest floor.

These predatory ants have lost their eyes over the course of evolution, but navigate themselves using their keen sense of smell and touch. driver ants have the largest colonies of any social insect, numbering between 2-22 million ants per colony.

These silent assassins are nomadic, and have been known to disintegrate any animal life in their path. driver ants attack by swarming. The effect of a swarm is so devastating, that animals as large as elephants have been known to flee their path. They do not rely on stingers to attack but rather they use their large and powerful mandibles to create puncture

wounds and tear off sections. driver ants have even been known to kill animals with hard exoskeletons, by gnawing at the soft joints to gain entry, before eating their prey from the inside out.

All the ants in a colony are female. However, only one of them, the Queen, is responsible for breeding. She lays 1-2 million eggs every month, almost continuously. The Queen driver ant gets sperm from the bizarre male driver ant, which is a large winged insect known as a sausage fly. The sausage fly flies from one colony to another in order to stumble upon an ant highway. Once it does, its wings are removed and it is taken back to the nest where it is used as a sperm donor. The driver ant is Africa's deadliest killer.

"Winning people surround themselves with inspirational, infectious types who are always positive and proactive."

Very little of what we achieve in life is as a result of a completely solo effort. We are all surrounded by our support structures that guide us in one form or another. These individuals make up our team and are responsible for ensuring that our preparation is clinical, leaving nothing to chance. They help us eradicate complacency, remain humble, maintain perseverance, ensure sacrifice, constantly "raise the bar", and nurture a type of discipline and dedication that is in keeping with the spirit of champions.

"On every team, there is a core group that sets the tone for everyone else. If the tone is positive, you have half the battle won." – **Chuck Noll**

The African driver ant may seem small and insignificant, but as a colony they best emphasize the saying: *"As individuals we are strong, but together we are invincible"*.

COMPASSION

A feeling of deep sympathy and sorrow for another who is stricken by misfortune, accompanied by a strong desire to alleviate the suffering

The Story of the African Elephant

The African elephant is the largest land mammal on earth, standing between 9-11 feet in height and weighing in between 8000-11000 lbs. The most prominent features on an African elephant are the extremely large ears and long tusks. The ears of an elephant help expel heat, whilst their long trunks are used for smelling, breathing, trumpeting and drinking. Their trunk alone contains about 100,000 muscles.

Male and female African elephants have tusks which are used to dig for food and water. In the males, these are also used for battle. These tusks are made of ivory, an extremely valuable material, which has endangered the lives of this species due to illegal poaching.

These social animals live in groups called herds, which roam great distances in search of roots, grass, fruit, and bark which makes up their daily diet. An adult elephant can consume up to 300 lbs of food a day.

The most remarkable and unique attribute of the African elephant is their understanding of death and the dying process. These elephants seem to comprehend the feelings and emotions associated with grieving, which are clearly exemplified in their behavior. If they notice a fellow elephant in trouble, their initial reaction is to help. If the elephant cannot be helped, members of the herd stay with the distressed elephant until the moment of their passing on. Even after this, they engage themselves in a long mourning process which involves touching the bones or body of the dead fellow elephant, and returning to the place of death to pay homage.

"You give but little when you give of your possessions. It is when you give of yourself that you truly give." — **Kahlil Gibran**

Compassion is wanting others to be free from suffering. It is a feeling that is born from empathy and is characterized by a burning desire to want to alleviate that suffering. The ability to be compassionate starts with the simple act of forgiveness. Forgiveness has the power to banish hurt and resentment, which leads to a more loving interactions and a holistic understanding of the feelings within your heart. These are the feelings that allow you to show compassion to not only humans, but animals as well, because true compassion is not discriminatory but all encompassing.

The frailty of life is always taken for granted in the animal kingdom where survival of the fittest and survival of the strongest are the general laws of the jungle. It is inspirational to see the mighty African elephant - the largest mammal on land – show such a deep understanding and emotional trauma at the loss of life.

"It is lack of love for ourselves that inhibits our compassion towards others. If we make friends with ourselves, then there is no obstacle to opening our hearts and mind to others." — **Anonymous**

Ingenuity

*The quality of being cleverly
inventive or resourceful*

The Story of the Elephant Shrew

The elephant shrew or sengi is an insectivorous mammal indigenous to Africa. These small animals have a brownish grey coat, mouse-like tails, a long pointed nose and rather long legs for their size. With an average size of 10-30 cm, these are not very social animals that live in monogamous pairs in a restricted territory, which they mark out using scent glands.

The legs of a sengi are directly underneath their body, making them rather unstable but quick. sengi's move in a hopping fashion much like a rabbit, which allows them to spring over obstacles when they are in danger. Their active lifestyle means they need to eat very regularly, which exposes them and makes them vulnerable to predators.

To counteract their vulnerability, the sengi develops an intricate network of paths and trails in their territory. This labyrinth of trails

is memorized by the sengi and kept free of twigs and shrubs, which could mean the difference between life and death. A sengi spends almost three quarters of its day running through these trails to ensure they are free from any debris in order to ensure the escape routes are clear in times of danger.

The elephant shrew is a tiny animal that has ingeniously developed a plan to outwit its enemies and ensure the survival of it's species in a geographical location that would otherwise have seen the extinction of the sengi. The ingenuity displayed by the sengi is what is required to flourish in this hostile territory.

"Invincibility lies in the defense; the possibility of victory in the attack." – Sun Tzu

Ingenuity is the art of seeking a victory before the battle has begun. It is the tactical dispensation of a strategic plan that is a combination of knowledge from your environment and an analysis of yourself. Ingenuity is simply all about doing the basics the best, which is a cornerstone fundamental in business and sport. The sengi has taught us that ingenuity and resourcefulness is all that's needed to overcome any obstacle.

"*The difficulties of life are intended to make us better, not bitter.*" – *Anonymous*

OPPORTUNITY

*A situation or condition favorable
for attainment of a goal*

The Story of the Komodo Dragon

Komodo dragons are the world's heaviest living lizards and are indigenous to the Indonesian Islands. These carnivorous animals can grow to an average length of 6-10 feet and weigh close to 175 lbs. Despite their size, they are fast moving and very agile.

Komodo dragons have a keen sense of smell, which allows them to seek out carrion up to 3 miles away. Like most monitor lizards, they can also climb trees and are exceptionally good swimmers. These ferocious animals definitely have a bite worse than their bark. The teeth of the komodo dragon are laterally compressed with serrated edges, which allow the dragon to tear off pieces of meat. If this is not bad enough, the mouth of the komodo dragon is full of virulent bacteria, which is guaranteed to kill its prey in under a week.

Komodo dragons are opportunistic scavengers and predators who will eat anything they can overpower. However, they most often move silently in bushes or lay in wait to ambush their prey. The komodo dragon has been known to kill prey as large as water buffalos by attacking the animal's legs. The komodo's bite will unleash their deadly saliva, which will kill the animal in a few days. During that time, a small group of the cannibalistic lizards will follow the wounded buffalo until it dies or is weak enough to overpower. The komodo dragon is a classic example of an opportunistic predator. These territorial lizards will seldom let another dragon onto its territory unless they are on a food run. The komodo dragon will almost always feed on animals that have already been killed by their counterparts, and if need be, will mostly hunt by catching their prey unaware and by surprise.

*"The opportunities to achieve our goals are so rare, that when they present themselves, we must give the fullest of which we are capable." – **Gary Player***

I was once told that luck is where opportunity meets hard work, but I think opportunity is where dedication meets discipline. Luck is just a by-product. "You can be good without working hard, but to be great you must work hard. And if you want to be better than your previous self, you have to change the way you do things." This is the mindset that will ultimately create opportunities. Seizing those opportunities could be the turning point in your life.

*"Opportunity is missed by most people because it is dressed in overalls, and looks like work." – **Thomas Edison***

VICTORY

A success or triumph over an enemy in battle or war

The Story of the Draco Lizard

The draco is a tree dwelling, insectivorous lizard indigenous to South-east Asia.

The draco is well known as "The Flying Dragon". This amazingly unassuming lizard has a magnificent arsenal of defense mechanisms. When threatened by predators, this 20 cm long lizard, will initially camouflage itself. It to fails, the lizard will take to the skies in its final attempt to escape.

The draco lizard when attacked, will run up a tree to its furthest point. From there, it will with a "leap of faith" jump off the tree. Its ribs and the connecting membranes can extend to create a wing, whilst its hind limbs are flattened to create a wing-like cross section. This enables the lizard to glide through the air, covering distances up to 195 feet, and ensuring a safe passage away from danger.

"Confidence helps people to take control of circumstances rather than be dragged along with them."
– Rosabeth Moss Kanter

Whilst fear is the single most daunting stumbling block in any person's career, confidence is the most fortifying building block in their development. It allows you to express yourself freely and reinforce trust, in both your skill and your strategy. Confident people are brave and believe in harnessing the positive energy that the universe has to offer. They have the power to take a 'leap of faith' against adversity simply because doubt has no place in their heart and mind.

Remember, *"If you are afraid for your future, you don't have a present." – James Petersen*

The wonderful draco lizard is a unique example of how the tiniest, most unassuming, and most insignificant creatures in the wild, have adapted survival mechanisms that almost always ensure victory in the face of adversity.

Life is a struggle, but victory is almost always attainable.

REFERENCES

1. The Art of War for Managers – 2nd ed Gerald A Michealson and Steven Michealson

2. The Prophet – Kahlil Gibran (1983)

3. Play your business like a pro – Anton Swanepoel and Gary Player (2005)

4. Secrets to Happiness – B.C. Forbes (2008)

5. Life: Extraordinary Animals, Extreme Behaviour - by Martha Holmes, Michael Gunton, Rupert Barrington, and Adam Chapman (2010)

6. David Attenborough's Life Stories – David Attenborough (Audio CD 2010)

7. Animal: The Definitive Visual Guide to the World's Wildlife – David Burnie & Don E. Wilson

8. All definitions extracted from www.dictionary.com

NOTES

NOTES

NOTES

NOTES

NOTES

NOTES

NOTES

NOTES

NOTES

NOTES

NOTES

NOTES